LEO CONNELLAN

PROVINCETOWN
AND OTHER POEMS

CURBSTONE PRESS

Printed in the U.S. by BookCrafters on acid-free paper
cover illustration by Michael McCurdy

Curbstone Press is a 501(c)(3) nonprofit publishing house whose
operations are supported in part by private donations and by
grants from ADCO Foundation, J. Walton Bissell Foundation,
Inc., Witter Bynner Foundation for Poetry, Inc., Connecticut
Commission on the Arts, Connecticut Arts Endowment Fund,
Lannan Foundation, LEF Foundation, Lila Wallace-Reader's
Digest Literary Publishers Marketing Development Program,
administered by the Council of Literary Magazines and Presses,
The Andrew W. Mellon Foundation, National Endowment
for the Arts-Literature, National Endowment for
the Arts International Projects Initiative and The Plumsock
Fund.

Many of these poems appeared in *Another Chicago Magazine,
Abiko Quarterly, Die Young, Hermes' Crossing, Negative
Capability, The New York Quarterly, New England Review/
Bread Loaf Quarterly, New Virginia Review, The Pucker Brush
Review,* and *Vietnam Generation.*

Library of Congress Cataloging-in-Publication Data

Connellan, Leo.
    Provincetown, and other poems / by Leo Connellan.
        p.   cm.
    ISBN 1-880684-29-2 (trade paper) : $11.00
    I. Title.
    PS3553.05114P7   1995
    811'.54—dc20   94-23591

published by
CURBSTONE PRESS
321 Jackson Street
Willimantic, CT 06226

contents

this book is for
Henry Anderson and James Connellan
my father-in-law and my father

NO, THE RIVER NEVER FRIGHTENED ME

On the other side of the river
all we anticipate here and are not there
to find it is not there either to have
or we are not good enough here or there.
There here where we are is the other side,
two visible sides of a river each
invisible. Blue ice is breaking up.
Ice cubes of sky shined on by bright sun.
Then a frown of dark cloud. Suddenly
the river looks like it has a crack in it,
gurgling blue water rattle.
In Spring the wind over this water
is roses of perfume and young excitement.
The river is to splash in, laugh in and what
lies on the other side of the river doesn't
concern us because whatever danger is subtle,
even invisible. Even drowning seems
an accident, not intent. Throughout
Summer and Fall there is warmth and color
and we are alive in ourselves. Then
dark silver spreads frozen and
we can run and walk on top of water, still,
never do we get off on the shore on the
other side of the river nor does
anyone from over there come among us
until ice cracks fill us with wonder
and fear that we are being forever left yearning
malcontent, fearing and cowardice unfulfilled.
I am here from over there, here perhaps alone
until I hear from you. I was excited to go
skating and over splitup and crackup. No, the
river never frightened me. I am in search of a poem.

MOTEL

I

We came in off the Parkway past two
union pickets silent in their shivering behind
signs since Reagan and The Air Transporters.

This is a new one from the most famous luxury chain,
just opened, with a special cheap rate to fill
rooms and give staff practice...that

succeeds because the help's picked from immigrants.
Cocktail waitress forced to wear outfit that
makes her look stripped, fired if they catch

her chewing or her mouth looking like it's got
anything in it but her tongue. Athletic teams,
Corporations hoping that false front if not their

products gets business will fill this place,
depression outside or not. Starving human
beings within a mile or not.

Poverty is within walking distance of this place
up little oil dirty snow side streets here. Hunger
shows in the punctured tattered half drawn

window shades and in the cold pipes without heat.
Murder just to eat and for something warm, a scarf to
clutch around your adam's apple and try not to

think of the numbness of the rest of your body
lonely so cold, to control rage at being so cold
and unfilled while just across the street

this new motel has human beings who can
spend and do not even pause once in
mid-swallowing of good Grand Marnier

cutting the insides of their throats like
smooth honey, as some just across the
street consider cutting the outside of

their throats with steel; not once
in this opulence does a guest shudder
thinking of poor men who cannot fill

those they love or themselves with any
good things and even consider let alone
do anything about it...There is a

toughness in the breezes. All around this place
is the quiet of hard struggle and to
walk here is not safe....If they think

you might be some big money from the motel
you have asked a starving man for your life
and he'll take it for his life.

II

Here I was in a luxurious room with room service
and a balcony, but the maids in the hall when
I passed them saw penury in the set of my mouth fixed

forever in fatigue and endurance's look and
on their hands and knees scrubbing carpets
and the halls of the motel hallways, if they wanted

their jobs, one or two of these lovely ladies smiled
at me enjoying that one of them had somehow managed
to be a guest, and if I had wanted to imagine

that I could get away with being anyone but
who I am, a sweeper like them, their knowing
smiles as I passed them told me I fooled no one.

I was like an elderly trick passing Queens thinking
that growing old ever hides your soul, that
you're "everybody's make"...no it wasn't sly suggestion

their smiles and looks knowing me, no, it wasn't that
their postures on their hands and knees forcing
their bottoms to elevate as if they'd do anything in

my mind for a twenty dollar bill, no there was no
offer, even if growing old I yearned for there
to be one more offer...just one more! Once more

heads turned cruising me—no matter my fantasy
wishes, there was nothing more in that hallway
than my dirty images and just one or two

worn out human beings knowing
another when they
saw one...

III

I was so common and familiar
in my conversations with desk clerks
that when the elevator was tied up

by maids moving their carts
from floor to floor, they had
no problem suggesting

I use the Service elevator which meant walking
through their kitchen passing garbage and through
their laundry room to ride with the Room Service

waiter who knocked on my room door with reverence, now
a knit brow disturbed frown as he really saw me now
next to him riding up in his shit, and though

he was young and couldn't put it together, he too
sensed I was more an older him than a guest here
yet he knew in seconds as the Service elevator

got me to my floor, he would have to resume
catering to me. I'll always wonder if he suddenly grew up
in that realization...

IV

The desk clerks knew only too well
I was in their motel on an ingenious low rate
plan...you dial 800 information and ask

for the package number...owing everyone but
life gets so pressed you blank your conscience
temporarily of the people you telephoned

in horror about the wage garnishee and phone turnoff
if they didn't rush you money...but if
you don't do this you won't live to pay them back, worse,

you won't be alive to be the person they sent cash.
Man has to escape out of his cages for
new breath...I....just....did it!

There isn't any excuse to do what you wish when you owe!
But I did it to survive and not use or drink
or have a coronary for principle.

Should this make me disreputable, dishonorable,
at least I can be told this personally
and not through the grass of my tomb....

...and up in the hallways thickly carpeted like
bath towels the maids on their hands and knees were
washing carpets and the walls vulnerable

to my stare at their bottoms raised in air
strung out here along the hallway like so much
breathing meat bereft of their dignity as

they put out their flesh for food and roof. We motel guests
gorged and drank as if poverty were not
close death whispering dying along

the bedposts of luxury. Evil dressed its best.
Poverty had started to harden us beyond
the ability to ever enjoy again, but at

this motel that succeeds because the help's picked
from immigrants, I saw a chinese or vietnamese woman
maid all expression of joy erased from her naturally

stoic disposition, blank, only her mouth
without even her lips moving let words, like
hollow echoes from a pebbled well, out if

spoken to; she was desperate lest one
of her answers lose her this work....This
small vietnamese or chinese woman she

seemed to appear out of the walls, probably a
service elevator as I would come and go in
and out of our room...pushing a heavy long

cart with everything on it to make rooms up
just about all this little tiny woman could push
by people like me there for comfort and pleasure

from our new depression given us for our faith and
vote by our President for being the fools we
always are always allowing the lie that it's

the Welfare Indigent not the wealthy who are
responsible for our loss of jobs, pensions
medical help...soon the years you can

still climb three flights of stairs on two sides
of twenty one buildings if you have to and
sweep one all the way down and climb up the next

or do anything but sit in the corner
of some Reagan club soup kitchen shelter
will be gone...of course

I'm to blame
but dying isn't easier because
you deserve it....

TOMORROW

Tomorrow is like yesterday
resented, resisted. Now
frightened of time when
everything could be done

for us, we fear imagination
so why are you surprised
you cannot cope with imagining
the old Hormel, Armour Ham

plants becoming refleshing
plants, you'd have to go
before age 35 or you'd be
too old, the skin of your

skeleton too set to de-skin,
then you refleshed with new
kidneys, liver, heart so
you'll always look young.

Man and computer cure paraplegia,
now they can part whole spine
from body long enough to bypass
nerve connection...cars become

heli-cars, combination car and
helicopter. Parking now off the
ground within your hovering
space inches above each other and

get down on the ground and back up
into your heli-car by pliable
pogo spring ladder. Now
you get ceiling as well as

wall to wall tv all going
at once, watch with a twitch
turn of your neck side to
side and up and down and

so as not to get afflicted
with "twitch turn neck" a
prevalent disease, especially
back at the beginning when

all the marvels became available,
you skim look quick left and right
up, down or straight ahead or
settle on one tv show to watch like

they did in the old days. Laser
surgery means nobody's body ever
gets cut. Everything gets done
for us, we get bored...but

there's a new game around, everybody's
doing it, it's called reading, thinking and
I tell you when you start your eyes
water, come together, almost cross, your

head aches trying to do this what they
call concentrate and you find out
that with all the wonderful everything
man ever dreamed for you've now got, you

don't have yourself, you've lost yourself,
can't think, reason, read, agree
disagree, there is no hopeless
struggle you have to surmount, so

what good is being renewed, reskinned,
living a couple of thousand years!
The sky's up there, we've always
been able to see it and we

cut a way through its heat shield
out into weightless whatever...but
we have to use ourselves here
and out of gravity.

LETS FALL IN LOVE

My mother was an abortion.
No, I mean it, an unborn fetus
eggs planted in a hippopotamus
so if I seem an animal
there's this good reason
but I'm empty from not knowing
my real mom who was never here
so I could be anti social or distant
or in so much need I'm overwhelming.
Should I love my birth mom or mom mom?

STOCKBRIDGE, MASSACHUSETTS

Outside Red Lion Inn room 240
snow flakes touch Norman Rockwell canvas
Stockbridge, Massachusetts, loose in air like
specks of frosting on this cake town saved
from looking like a Saturday Evening Post cover
by flesh, breathing people, real life, not neat
scenes with no problems...I locked my car
and couldn't get back in and a Policeman kind,
gracious but tired, weighed by what lies under
tinsel, used a tool that looked like a thin saw
with hooks to catch the inside lock down a
window without breaking the door so I couldn't
open or close it, and I could move again.
Hawthorne, Bryant, LongFellow, this Inn you stayed in
doesn't exist. The carpeted rooms creak and their
carpets and fixtures suggest and hint trails you
traveled, some no wider than a path between
communities suddenly cleared and lived in among
forest, roads, dirt, no wider than for a stage
coach to travel, enough for human feet and horses
and wheels, are now wider roads paved for our
transportation; beautiful in the Berkshires where
ice sparkles on tree branches when light rain freezes
and what is vanished is visible but the light of candles
flickering imagination is now electricity and no one
knows what a Thunder Mug is, you pull a chain and
refuse is gone, in a bathroom not out back or down a
hall or left for someone else to have to carry swishing
to dump, become immune to vomiting. The old Inn
you knew has been added onto once moving about was
solved but age only hides the youthful face which
if you look you can see for yourself without need of photos.
Once human beings in these rooms dreamed of perfecting, a
day when somehow buildings would be built so tight, solid

against weather as to erase noise. Now in our hustle
and clutter we pay for creaks when we walk across rooms
off balance as if creaking unites us with those whose
breath breathed in these rooms which now heave from
hanging on, shifted in this ancient building by rage
of wind and storm but have television now; Room Service
and the old Inn has an elevator, however the beds and food
are good and if you were here today you'd gladly stay over.

YORK MAINE

For Theodore Junkins

Through the Cutty Sark motel room 21 picture window now
the gray waves coming into York Beach like
an invasion of plows pushing snow. Tomorrow
the sun will scratch its chin and bleed along the skyline
but today everything is gray poached in a steam of fog.
Inedible Sea Gulls, domesticated by human charity,
obliviously peck the land sweeping around like a
sprung fish chowder of rocks of vanished summer
when the outsider empties his pockets here for relief,
fresh salt air, the silence, soothing sleep.
Junkins Country here up the old Berwick road 91
past Mcintyre Garrison built against Abinakis and
Moody's actual church used as a barn now, Junkinses
intermingled with Pines and this earth is Junkins earth.
The Junkinses are spread around the woods here
in little graveyards, beware of hunters if you
try to find their resting places. At Scotland Bridge road the
great stone arch with the name Junkins chiseled out of rock, an
arch of stone all by itself like an entrance to a great
castle but only to a mud rut farm house road with little boys
standing tall and ready to spring if they have to, looking curiously
at you by their swinging tire from a string wondering what
you see in piled rocks they see every day...hardly! Perhaps they
do know that Moody lies within steps of their yard, Moody of the
shooting accident so he did not wish to show his face to men again.
On a day like this the dead seem to appear. They
were here alright! Blue is overcome by gray
Sepia gray, Umber gray, raw Sienna, burnt Sienna.
Gray seems no color at all. You see it, but how
together? I can come to the under colors.
if I could find it, I could find the answer to life

to what to expect. God's energy, the day's changes,
clouds like a veil, and then the sky clear blue
as if this world has no other color, the sea
just exploding here

THE TREACHERY OF FLAME

Something has changed us, the wild grapes.
Excitement is in other imaginations of our taste,
to keep wish for us. Now we have been seen, fingered,
and picked over. We have squirted whatever we had,
the market is crowded, so to stand out one must
be impossibly rare. We have merely been the
new blossoms who come along, show and are gone.

AN IMAGE FROM HOWARD COUGHLIN

Thinking of lines I will not write
joys my inner heart for poetry.
None of us live long enough to think
and inspiration rarely comes, it is
in you or it isn't, but plagiarism
permeates everywhere and those
who would fail students do it.
Recently talking with a brilliant learned friend
I mentioned a terrible woman I know,
evil, who destroys souls, to
Doctor Howard Coughlin who instantly
recognized the sort, responding
"People like her like her" and
I knew that if I work to find a line like that
there will be someone I will never meet
not yet born or conceived who will read.
It's worth all the work, the hopeless depression.

SLOUGHTER POET

Let me always live
in a sloughter community
ostracized by truly
European origin. The
world is mixed but hearts are one.
I am a poet, a neglected
despised people, call me
a sloughter, please, it is
only my poems that may
amount to much and they may
if you will them to out of your
own disturbance bringing
to them your imagination of what
they convey, not mine, a sloughter poet
at best in all the Five Points slums
of the earth seeping sewage around me
only masked by the pleasant looking
architecture of men, but really
the grave, eternity is always
breathing foul above ground
smothered by perfumes, but only
the heart's inner mix of brotherhood
is worth this life.

CHILDREN OF YOUR HORROR EXISTENCE, MANHATTAN

New York, there is a sudden overwhelming
rushing feeling that everything
is going to burst.
Children mug and kill in rage
that anyone should be graceful and
cultured while they starve.
There is no ambition where there
is no opportunity.
Distorted and forced abuse, their
joy, their fun. No one is going
to come along for them. They
are not going to come along for us.
New York, there is a sudden overwhelming
rushing feeling that you might come apart.

HUNGER

The subways are free of graffiti. Now
that cute little boy Cherubic is
riding to hurt people in Central Park or
hustling unsuspecting women off train
up dark track to tear their pants down
praying to survive a plunge that stings
and his sour breath. Their comprehension
there spread out up on all fours fanny high
elevated to be entered by threat suddenly aware
something is inside them where they never
considered it could be in the gasping fright
of expecting to die and realizing within
the quick excited back and forth plunging,
jerking in and out in and out smack in a fit
like the fit of a plumber's friend that they're
tolerating it but finding themselves
still alive. Their inside souls think they are
forever killed by what they did not know could
happen to them or did know and rather than
never see God's face would prefer death, dying
there on the dark cold tracks but he is gone
and they are left staggering in a madness of the
loss of themselves suddenly without knowing why
and an inability to commit suicide.
Suddenly offered urge. They tell Police we've been
sodomized by a Cherubic child but it doesn't interest,
enrage, impress in this time of AIDS when
everyone can die from a tongue kiss, the child from
the mother's mouth who trusted her
lover, thought he was discreet but
death is become tired of foolish risk.
Cherubic is unseen by us, not as clear
as graffiti which disturbed us but
we were unconsciously conscious. Now

our stomachs don't churn in this new
cleanliness in which Cherubic looks just
like a child walking and blowing gum out
of tree lined neighborhood where flowers bloom
and trash cans sit in tidy rows, coming to
sit across from us, boxed in victims of necessity,
sprawled with his legs apart the way gawky
kids do, you can gasp in your urge
at the shadow against his young short pants.
It is hot from thinking about unknown strangers...who
will he be sticking it in this time after he
clubs them or slits their throats or puts it in
a way that puts them away, he knows intuitively
makes them like him. Cherubic victims will wander
life comatose or in therapy or become seducers of
other innocents...many a decent husband will
cringe whimpering for his ass like house pet cats
meow for their food which they think they've got
coming from raging women used and scorned and never
able to find Cherubic...and we rock with him to and fro
on this subway train off which insanity has been erased.

HOT DAY IN NEW YORK

It is crowding 98 without air, too hot
for love, lust craves egg creams. It is
the season of Con Edison and poor people
who struggle for light, electricity.
Now is shut off threat. Somehow
ruthless winter cold killing you seems
more barbaric than summer 98 degrees humidity
so law prevents shutoffs in snow and cold
but now your back bill comes before ice.
Even the wealthy become human like everyone else now.
Millionaires in fascinated fear of the unknown,
being without money, invite a spectacle to their
billionaire parties to tell everyone what
it's like to sleep with eviction gnawing and
wake wondering how you'll even eat on Monday
the first day of the week, let alone all week
when Con Edison means it they'll turn off
all your electricity, forget air conditioners,
you can't see and, broken, reach them out
your sweat crumpled dollars sobbing "let there be light!"
hoping the shut-off from which there may be no return
hasn't happened yet if you hurry with your money and
outside the oblivious millionaire's isolation his chauffeur
must inform him of the humps of New York created by
the genius who laid steam pipes under the streets of Manhattan
in the late 19th century which combined with hot sun will get
your car trapped by bumps in the road that form asphalt
softened like syrup reshaped hardens into car devastating hummock...
....life in summer New York is heat rashes in your crotch in
overcrowded bewilderment sticky and stuck.

THE $100 STREET PERSON

Corporations, government, th'people we vote for are
firing us fresh supplies of street person.
Don't worry! Forget the Japanese cows, we'll never
be out of meat. Th'legendary Hemstead himself
comes from 9th avenue to see to it personally
th'humans feel good, fed, stuffed warm, stimulated,
massaged, squeezed in airshaft, crammed in tight
as possible until they almost can't fit, to develop
fatter tissues by forcing gallons of beer and food into him
constantly giving him rubdowns, even ejaculating
him so he feels sperm ejected smooth in far off
memory fantasy, since of course, it took kidnapping, being
a human who comprehends and can decide he didn't just agree, so,
Hemstead, everybody's sorry, wants him to feel as good about
this as possible until it's time to club him stunnin' sudden in
airshaft abbatoir so blood congeals and he tastes good.
Hey! Sylvester'll probably be in Hemsteads this week to eat
this sweaty tasty answer to clearing our streets of failed flesh.
Jacky Greasy used to sit...over there in th'corner in
Hemstead's sippin' his Brandy Alexanders...Thisis, you know,
for th'money New Yorkers to who a hunnert dollars isn't kleenex.
People who got lotsa money, time, nothin' new, nothin' happenin'!
Itsa experience! Everything in New York is a shot. Buster
Douglas was gone in a shot. Last year Hemsteads, th'famous
steak house served fork melting tender Japanese cow.
Now look what we got!

HOME AGAIN

Henry Powell's car broke down in the Bronx.
He was off the falling apart Parkways
with pot holes that almost keep the
wheels that fall in them and, pulled up
and out, throw cars out of line, to
cut through neighborhood. He wanted
to see what was left of where his
Grandfather settled, now stripped shells,
hollow buildings with too many holes in them
for echoes. The skulls were out in their skin heads
and four or five walked around his car, pulled
machine pistols and made sure he stayed
in the neighborhood.

JAZZ

A groan of brass looking for a note
that sounds like phlegm in a throat
almost giving us lust and the escape of smoke.
The horn has a thing with tin
if tin has a thing with a horn.
We hear what we want to hear
soul moan, not scales, man don't
play scales if you're not Coltrane.
Real horn men risk, when everyone's
playing loud, fast, covering, Miles Davis
blowing slow found us where
we were lost and brings us back.

SHOOTER

Hey Momma I'm going to know Brooklyn
just because we live here. Nothing's happening,
dying is living, so we drive by and and shoot because
nothing is ours, you don't destroy yours.
Sometimes we hit and sometimes we get hit. A
bullet just rolled off my roof. You go to
Columbia University, I go to the undertaker.
I explain the bullet I keep on my dresser to
my momma she worry more than she already
thinkabout...so don't tell her I'll be here
until I'm not...oh, Momma you birthed us abandoned
by men, any man, a couple of steady sleepovers who
could buy shoes, food, clothes to keep coming. You
did what you could for us and now all you got
for it is headstones.

SQUIRREL SHOOT

We would have nothing to do and great beauty
goes blind too close to our eyes. We would walk
through dark, quiet woods on afternoons when
sun shafts trailed the dried pine needle forest
floor, and we had the great manhood of guns
with us, in country too peaceful, as life is flowing
sudden actions, and mammal with a brain destroys
by nature, having to set up protection against himself.
The loins that produced us were snoring,
buzzing flies heaving from their breath,
our mothers lost to us the instant
we felt the instinct of our difference.
High in the trees, the Squirrels would suddenly
jolt in their tree to tree springing, as our guns
crashed against the fragile ribs of their life, dropping
them to our feet of exultation, like great laughter gone limp.
Until we were, then, no longer boys, come to know that
Squirrels should live and Deer and Fish and you and me.

WINTER

Look at lakes, now shattered mirrors meld.
Water we have sunk in holds us up.
See! Evergreens over there! While some
hardwood, Maples, Elms seem death bent but
as sure as thick white snow is frozen water webbed,
birds will be back in those trees replenished in green leaf.

PULLING OAR

Every January my hands
still blister, callous over as
they did each year I was number 4
of engine rooms, rowing's
power to throw Coxwains
overboard and take the shirts
home off backs of Crew fallen
exhausted over their oars like
stacked flat pancakes, beaten.
Fresh water, salt water, polluted
water, makes no difference; lakes,
rivers, bays, canals, irrigation
ditches, wherever there is enough
width, length. The water rowed on
effects how the race is rowed, how
boats are rigged but we'll row
anywhere any time sweating,
fearing "catching a crab" which
means the force of the boat moving
forward may cause the oar to turn
under water; in my sleep I dread
catching a crab a place like
Onodonga Lake or even a smaller
Eastern Sprint like in Worcester.
Pulling oar, that lust, urge needed
to part water without speedboat blade, our
common secret wish to be the best
we can make ourselves...until,
in the sweat of stroke, we are
in it and the water
of our sweat is dropping
into the water of competition.
Everyone counts, every
stroke together, the

crackling ripple of our
shoulder muscles stops
the very wind's face as
we depend on correct rhythm
of our Cox's call; if she or he is
off at all it can kill the stroke
of our heart's attempt.

THE SHADOW OF A LEAF

I

We lie into disintegration underneath leaves
if we are not cremated and scattered
when our breath has gone back to the air.
It is as if we are in a never realized Portrait;
our breathing prevents the finished picture,
and without our breaths something isn't in it.

The fixtures, houses, meadows, fences, trees
thick and hazy, vast magnificent view
are there forever for the wonder of next humans
unless Nuclear removes them. In rage of our
inner instincts suggesting to us that the world
is a vacuum area we fill until we don't, revolt

at our recognition of this but helpless,
seems to become inner fury turned cowardly vengeance.
We kill because removing from among us seems
the worst we can do to anyone. Yet what do you call
what you do with no certain result!? Who can hurt
what is knocked out? We only know how much we cling

to this space we're in, how we don't want to leave
this unfinished ever changing earth, yet we
even kill children whose lack of life experience, perception;
seeing violence attracts death defying behavior that
seems exciting not ever believing they can die...only
old people die...We have no wish to watch

and retch on smell burning stench or to see hanging.
The moment they kick you out whirling a rope,
sinking, he fell through himself with a snap.
His life burst shut off blood through the skin

of his face like a bruised purplish plum.
Needles with overdoses, life goes in a tremble

as soul tries to creep by interrupted heart rhythm
in silent cleanliness without odor, seemingly
unviolated human on a rolling cart as if asleep
but never to wake as we exhale our imagining
he's suffered by vanishing before we do.
We know he's lost his life but what a let-down

after we've taken it, we can never be sure what is sure!
If, indeed, eternal paradise is our reward for dying, then
why kill a man into eternal joy! The man now dead is unable
to conceive punishment. Since not one of us is or
ever has been dead, we cannot know if we really deprive him.
Fear become a thrill of sending someone there without

our going, the nearest we can come to this fear of ours.
We are watching ourselves die...and will we die for our
sins or Paradise...? He is now seeing what I'm fearing to see.
He is now seeing what I'm denied to see, so, in this
moment of his death is envy...even in the act of vengeance
you escape me in your knowledge now and I wish

I could call you back for a moment, rip
tombstones to ask you, burst your coffin and give you
your life in exchange if I must to ask
you not did it hurt but what do you know now...
The blind dread what they cannot touch.
We who can see do not see at all.

II

You invite me to lunch, I think you
mean me to present myself at your front door,
ring the bell or rap my knuckles and

you'll beckon me into a fine sitting room
where we will have refreshment and chatter
before my salivating expectation is led
to its satisfaction. But no, I come

to your front door, but you block
my entering, standing with a picnic basket slung
on your arm like a trunk of gluttony
and you're carrying a big blanket. "Come," you
tell me and we go out back of your house
to a rather rough rock clumpy green cow pasture.
There are even cows here and there.

"Sit," you instruct me. You throw out the
blanket like a charade to a non-existent on coming bull
and, as for all the lucky, it settles for you
well enough. "Sit," you say, "we'll eat! I've
got good cold wine and chicken. I wanted
you to have lunch with me on this old pasture
because a very famous battle was fought here.

"Look how flies still hover buzzing, not just
over cows and us but expecting.
How warm serene the green is here under the sun.
But once men butchered each other right here,
blood rushed the gasps of hope.
This picnic blanket grass
was bayonet death's green.

III

"Come now, let us go inside, serenity is freezing.
Yes, sit, look out the window in this room of the living.
Now sit, listen, hear! Ghost shadows will always
materialize and vanish where telephone wires carry

our living voices still, underneath the electric hum
is the chorus of all those who lie forever in earth and

"where they've gone the buttercup they've become
does not tell, nor can you and I but picnic here.
All the actual that took place is happened
without consulting us and we can only imagine
out of imageries, Television, our dreams of
remembrances we are not even aware we ever noticed."

We can only assume we know what took place
as we give to all told tales our individual
identity's response. All our answers lie
in search and if we ever get a glimmer
of why human carcasses were birthed to forever
fight stink and for cleanliness, it is, truly,

as if somehow very procreation was to live to grow
up for death, dying. The God we live by wants us
created, it seems, to die for His Eternal Paradise...
Why is it told that "He" came to us, here on
our earth to grotesquely die, as if we asked Him to, what
say did we have in what must be done so we could be

saved from an unseen unknown Forever! Just what
occurred in this place Eden that we don't get AIDS for today, and,
sacreligious, we are assured on television that we've
"been to Mass" if we just watch it on Channel R, a soft
soothing washer woman voice reassures us that we are
not to worry about losing our immortal souls

if we watch Mass, the TV show. After, we can, apparently,
be and do as we wish, blinding ourselves, blocking out that
Eternal Hell is supposed to await us if we grapple
with and give in to doing and thinking everything
and anything we like as lust, desire urges....What on earth
will dear Christ have to do next time He comes

to win us Paradisiacal Forever, jump out of a plane aflame
as old time Rockers "The Grateful Dead" sing
"They Know Not What They Do" and land unhurt so
we'll believe it's really "Him," instead of
bringing Lazarus back, He Himself does such another trick
in our sophisticated age as to quickly win us back to

purity from scepticism but what is this!? Why must
"He" come to us again if "He's" already been here!
Why is "We must have faith!" screamed into us from
a first message in our umbilical cords if "He's"
been here! It's like telling children, don't
take a cookie I'll be watching when they know

in their confused little heads that you've left
the house. They've got Authority Figure, the
Keeper of Hair-brushes for their cherubic fat
bare bottoms if they answer back or ask
"how can you see me if I take a cookie if
you're not home?"...Oh, you who have gone, call back!

Whisper! Come to us in our most secret sleep.
Tell us what you know now....
If this Christ died for my sins did Christa McAullife
die for propaganda too!? Last time "He" rose from
the dead, that was stunning, before Space Craft
which "He" allowed us as if being willing to beat

his best earthly feats if it will get us to believe
what we cannot know or call back about to those who doubt,
think death is dead and dust and that's it.
Why did "He" come? What was necessary to insist
on making us with brains, feelings, reason only
to vanish no one knows where, it seems

almost genius to be cremated like
dust thumbing itself at dust but in
an urn and forever possible to have the jar you're in
picked up by a living hand and waved to the world,
that always seemingly never complete picture because
you're not in it and never ever were but look alive

physically on earth always looking caught yourself, your
image caught in some camera photo but only the temporary
person within, existing on this earth and vanishing, to be
looked at a hundred years in future by eyes who know
human beings photograph differently several times in any
week or day of their supposed lives as if we are never meant

not ever really to be seen as we really looked by anyone...ever
as if we truly in God's scheme, we're never here but just
flesh on skeletons allowed for awhile
The Devil's hope, excitement, anticipation
as if these really exist, but the second we're
satisfied we forget yearning.

Here you are only the temporary person in meadows
and jammed shopping Malls you and those of the past
and of future, always keeping the great canvas called
the world like an unfinished picture, all the
totally finished work is in the basement of the
earth's museum, graves. Finally putrified, then

dust to materialize into you, supposedly
in God's Paradise...But do we!? No one who has gone
tells us. Sometimes at night if we walk out in
deep bitter cold a sense of something trying to touch us
chills us more and in warm climates too this feeling comes
in the low key humidity, that the wind, soothing or even

extreme silence is trying to touch us, get our attention
with a message, information...is it from you who are gone?

What did we do!? Execute the bad into where the good go,
where we're supposed to go when we vanish from where
we now sit looking out at such serenity of life and color
and wish in the emptiness. Cremated, at least the urn

we are in is forever possible to see again and pick up
off our small safe graveyard shelf above ground.
Here once was I and am now dust but visible forever, not
sinking in earth's stink skeletal and looking like
no one but everyone, yet as we leave this life
it is wished we would not hush but tell

what we know now. Life is quiet.
We make all the noise there is in the world.
Otherwise, without our noise
the earth is as quiet as earth. Here in this house now,
we can look at vacancy though it appears
rich fields and flowers and knowledge

of what has happened here can seem to make a permanence and
a continuance but if only those who have been
could tell us what they know.
As we leave this it is wished
we would not hush but
tell what we know now.

IV

These once ploughed fields left suddenly, as if
the Farmer was called out west where he went.
But Scotland, Connecticut grew wild trees, roots
over Herbert Smokler soil turned to grow not to
vanish in weeds like snakes in insane hair.
Here, a grave dug with no committees met to say

you couldn't stay in the very earth ground of your
whole life but must be put in a prescribed meadow
with everyone you never knew. Well, you never ever
spoke to them anyway, so your silence
will always be normal, usual, though
you are buried away from what made

sense in your living at all "forever." You
are gone forever. What do you know!? It must
be all right or everyone would not allow
nondescript removal....Please at least call back!
you can't?...then...hint what you know, eery even
in what we think comes to us when a door slams.

Imagining is only concluding from an unknown noise
or sight or something put to us we think we
understand like the Carnival Barker's descriptions.
Life's circuses making us think we see a dangerous show,
thrilling to the sight, so give us a hint what
Eternal Paradise is or isn't. We're disappearing anyway!

Hint what you know. I know what you know! No
I don't but I think I do but thinking I do know
does not make it all right with me to leave, no. Could
flesh on us hold up two hundred years, a thousand, Forever!?
What would we have to take to preserve our carcasses
where we're used to being, right here, I want to

stay right here where I know fright and feeling
and can recognize that I enjoy at least the
idea of lust and it isn't dark. Noise is insinuation
and undoubtedly wrong concluding, but one can think,
one can see others, we can think we know
what's around the corner and where we've been.

V

Underneath leaves that pirouette before they
drift to become crisp on top of the ground
easily crushed into disappearance, they
fall smartly alive but finally crumble to vanish.
All the bright colors they were drawn from, the
unpainted picture, into brown crushed frozen

in cold autumn, the victims of cold as we lie
underneath the earth they are gone from too, if
we are not cremated or scattered to become
thoughts in heads of the living, often our features
almost materialize in human thinking as memory
recalls and puts our features to what is being remembered

We are the unknown faces in dreams good and disturbing,
people remember having after awakening and wonder who
the person so urgently communicating with them in their dream
was, it was us trying to call back what we know because
in the vault of human filing of experiences, observations
glimpsed in a flash, forgotten, filed somewhere

in regions of human brain undefined yet, we ourselves beg,
ask those who disappear to whisper to us in our sleep or
create scene in a dream of how this emptiness we fill
with despair and only by hoping, gets better somewhere! Where!?
...just in the shadow of a leaf, the beauty
the world made itself into from Glaciers

and eruptions is the end of our being in it, the
canvas, perhaps, the great landscaping of James Ruddock, yet
new people contemplating, mostly oblivious or where would
involvement, personal drive commitment ever come from of
me acknowledged and that whatever we do is for another's memory.
We are gone and no one can know if we need help...because we don't

call back...and in all our discoveries we must achieve
a way to call from here...*Hell is here knowing that*
we are born, developed, informed, experienced
and come to like and desire but leaving what we know!

Eden's real curse on us from a God who says
we bear guilt.

The leaves vanish but are in the buds of Hardwood...it is
only we who are here once and vanish, replaced
by the muscle that took purity in a garden and
must forfeit whatever life it initiates, doomed
and will not be here long. We are driven
to create what cannot survive but leaves, oh, call back!
                                        ...Beethoven where are you?

Statues, bridges, cathedrals last forever but they
who envisioned them and then drew sketches, designed
and built them in the never completed canvas earth are gone...forever.
Unless God has changed his mind, Planet travel in light years
takes only one of our earth life but the world goes by one hundred
years...perhaps, like toll booths, enough has now been collected of us.

GONE WALKING

I'll know where to find Donald Hall
and Mrs. Hall, drawn into their wild pasture
by heaven in its vacuum of us, down that
blue trail. They made sure to take that walk
in the Film and you see where you've been led.
There's a place like this for me where Thomaston,
Maine smells the blood lobster salt ocean
and my ancestors call for me through
lamenting fog horn. Mrs. Hall may be back
from that walk for awhile, as we are, but
soon the mountain and the pasture will
hold her invisible too...Now Donald
a smile and cold hard courageous eyes.

TREE SHADES

And the shadows point a finger
all over the earth, often grotesque.
Time has added silence
            except when the wind strikes up
conversation most of us
            are not attuned to hear.
Man has hung by the neck
            from a tree limb
and that is told by many branched fingers
            parting their hands
in futile shame.
Boys climb up to look over this world
            from the top.
They have to be grown men
            to start at the bottom.
One day
            looking down
from the highest pointing tree arm,
            they notice the shade it casts
and climb down to begin to
            search for it.

THE FROG JUMP AT LISBON CENTRAL SCHOOL

The children, dotting the grass like wild violets
and down in the play area worn bald by vanished shoes,
now orange markers for the Frogs to leap to
against Autumn's splashed colors.
On their hands and knees, other children pounding
the ground by the Frogs as if you had
two enormous sledge hammers with fingers
coming down each side of your ears exploding
dust so you jump for it, or are accidently
crushed under an excited undirected
hand or foot, leaping frantically until
it seems you've won yourself relief in
a can until you can be put back in a pond.

SMOKE TO COCHISE

It was the beginning of the end
            for us,
the end of us, Hickory Wood, not you.
            Apaches
outran horses. I go up three steps and collapse.
We are not close to the world any more
            but have taken the maiden lady
out of the earth.
            I could not rationalize
your burying a man up to his neck
and letting ants eat their way through syrup
to the meat of his face until his head
            was a fresh skeleton grimaced in its screams,
            until I took a job as a salesman
and worked with animals in business suits
            lying the naive housewife into a stroke.

LIFE

It's over,
smell, roses sweet, sweet
corn, the breath of breezes.
We lie unable to move
in dark grave where
there are no thrills
or they throw us ashes
that go nowhere yet all over
but is not seed.

THE OTHER MAN ON THE CROSS

To get Space Craft back into atmosphere
without burning up, it must come in
backward blunt and first absorb
the heat allowing it to evaporate a part
of capsule especially designed for boiling.
the earth is the place this was born,
ideas in human mind God put there
on the Cross into the head of the
man on his left who didn't ask
for paradise or even forgiveness;
he had his life and took his ending,
but dying, concentrated his thoughts
full of God's information put in them
as Calculous after Trigonometry after
Algebra for us to eventually
imagine through his
agonizing asphyxiation.

ALTERNATIVE

I

Bird takes flight
so Cat eats Mouse
Content in pause.

II

Bird takes flight while
Cat remains below
Content in paws.

BEFORE FIBERGLASS

Don Bragg, cheated, broken
as the 27 steel poles you snapped,
the sky of this earth is yours!
Astronauts know, Yeager knows
you were first up! Pole Vaulting is
a strength event and Bragg, 210, 6'4"
too heavy for Fiberglass. Compared
to 19' heights cleared with
Fiberglass poles, Bragg's 15' marks
seem little but it's like
complimenting an ice man or an elevator.
The ice man we don't see any more in our
electric freezing, ice man who ran up
five flights with a big block of ice on a
rubber mat thrown down his back like a vestment
with water creeping on the rubber like
colorless bleeding fingers down it, heavy on
his shoulders, to put the ice into
somebody's ice-box or an elevator
propelling him up to dump his block
of frozen water in a spring without
using much of himself, no involved sweaty
muscle to it, except to land right, not
snap an ankle...Bragg strictly propelled
from steel poles with little flex.

POEM WRITTEN IN THOMAS GRAY'S COUNTRY CHURCHYARD

Thomas Gray the trees too high now block
Stoke Poges view of Spires. Yet rich
green England never will erase. Sheep in
crew cut meadow still and cows not far off.
This graveyard always visioned bleak,
foreign to our imagining, yet your poem
touched us who could not see...almost
English velvety green garden.
Graves with a head-stone and
a foot-stone as though bringing
the conception of rest in
little beds.
The town in its pride of you, only survived
child of your mother, who wrote so
nobly for her, laid you to rest on top of your
aunt and your mother.
Does your noble homage cost you your own space.
The country here now is built up. Residential
across the street, empty fields gone. Pinewood
Movie Studio just down the road.
Fear we have lied to lies in us all. The paths of humility
lead to immorality, like yours, Thomas
Gray, if excellence and accomplished which astonishes
us throughout the ages, still matter in Nintendo now.
We who cannot write pleasing melancholy
still honor your heart that did. Your churchyard in
Stoke Poges is serene, after a war of bombing
and death and murder, still
we can see exactly
what you
saw, feel
what you felt.

OSCAR WILDE LAMENT

I THE GRAVE OF OSCAR WILDE

You lie not in England but among the French,
the Epstein Winged Sphinx of your tomb desecrated.
Something gouged the penis and testicles of stone
off the Winged Sphinx. Is it your "exquisite grotesque
half woman, half animal" come in form of English lady
to be certain the stone Sphinx is female? As "she
who loved Anthony and painted pharaohs" reminds
you want "that rare young slave with his pomegranate
mouth," not look to tourists who parade Père Lachaise
like a flying stud leaping through stone to mount any
maiden from the dark earth. No, out of doom, out of
ages something has said "Forever!" to us, to Epstein's
soul, no, you cannot undo what the earth has taken.
Perhaps you wished you were a lover of women, but you
loved the chameleon and the snake with loins and
hurt blue eyes that show pain will snuff them out.
Something, someone who knew well your "bestial sense
that would make you what you would not be," in physical
form of English woman crossed the channel and cut
your stone Sphinx and the way the testicles and penis
are chipped like razor sharp chisel powerfully
driven makes you shudder seeing a Ripper murder
or an ageless female Sphinx you wrote about who will
not let any mortal make her into a man even in stone.
She rides you still who loved Anthony and saw time begin.

II READING, BERKS

Just over the wall
of your Reading prison where
you wrote for a man being hung

hanged Hugh Cook Farringdon, Catholic Abbott
where The Holy Brook of The Seven Rivers
 of Reading ran

riches to threaten Henry the 8th's
throne, so he hanged
Hugh Farringdon

and now only the shell of ruined walls stands
soon to crumble and vanish forever,
just over the wall of Reading Gaol.

They have made the top
of the wall around Reading Gaol
round now

so that hooks of escape
cannot get a hold to lift
human spirit over.

And just over the wall of Reading Gaol
stands the biggest carved lion
of its kind in the world, yet

the lion's feet point the wrong way.
When this was pointed out to the artist
that no cat stands like that

he went and stood under
his work and
killed himself

where The Holy Brook
runs of The Seven Rivers
Of Reading....

...And so you died
of a broken heart, Oscar, yearning for
Westminster Abbey, at least a plaque like
Auden, but he didn't go to prison; your
head cracked by a guard's club in Reading Gaol,
shattering your hearing and your life young
to stumble Paris only a short while far away
from Frank Miles now and the culture your
wit sent chuckling from bedroom, theatre, cricket match.

MAINE

Here is dark blood green rich blue.
Sea Gulls, big bulbous freckled
red strawberries, blackberries burst
their bushes. Cold winter forces our
using ourselves. Summer will burn us
with its sun and run. Autumn hauls
bright Fall to brown dust. The sea
changes its colors at whim yet can
hit beaches furious, drawing back to strike.
The human here is lost in survival isolation.
Gnawing, always feeling we've left out something
we cannot define. Hunger is narrow irritability
with no time to philosophize in the sun baking
cold attitude that draws sighs of erotic delight
from tourists but ignores, betrays, kills its own; makes
us feel, though Maine cannot provide for its bright youth,
that we need an invisible passport if we leave, to
come back. There are potatoes here, big as beach balls!
Fish, Lobster, Clams, Sardines. If you're from Maine
your heart is here but nothing for you.

LOBSTER FISHERMAN

It's May-n-we gut th'lobster fever agin,
th'cold sea splashed freedom of hit but
computers make catchin' lobster such a
sure thing bringinin too many s'that
price drops and 's' not worth hit.
Once we had only a piece of rope and a weight
to find a ledge in th'sea leadin' from
shallow to deep water lobster come
to shed their shells so they can grow bigger
into our traps. Now anyone-n-everyone
with instruments that register depth and
ocean floor, technology takin' too much
until now th'thrill for doin' hit in wind
sea salt sand anticipation vanish.
Th'scavengers are saved by scavengers.

THE SUN

I

What blinds dark,
brights black, is
round light.

II

Letters I have agreed
make words we formed,
only three to spell
what takes darkness
out of the world.

FISH

We was coming in from catching
Scallops of violent water, the sea sucking
us under, boat sinking with Port in sight
so we all had to jump, helicopters
looking to find us somehow didn't
communicate with boat Coast Guard, so
Coast Guard boat sees us in the water and makes
us who are freezing from just being
pulled out of the ocean strip naked
on the deck, we need to be rescued
not finger probed...There's nuthin'
more hair raising than some seventeen,
eighteen year old youngster in a uniform
come at you waving a weapon could cut you
in two, the boy's eyes wild and in blinding
searchlight uncertain, you shivering wondering
if you shaking because they're making you stand naked
freezing, if you shaking can be misunderstood
as a move and the boy will waste you, it's
scary, something's got be done, they
try to tell us if we can fish, how many
days we can go out to fish and if we
crossed that there world court Hague line, means
like if you go into, say, Canadian water it could be
a hundred thousand dollar fine and our
licenses, the end of New Bedford! It
was hell then. They come on the boat
and rob us! Yes! They tell me to
stay back away from them while they
take a count of scallop meat and come out
too high... right there one of them
makes a phone call right in front of me

and they sell our catch! If I didn't
get that $17,000 back we're done in
Glouchester...we try not to break the law
...I've jettisoned scallops that might
make us over count. We sift them with a
milk crate throwing food, money back
into the sea...it's better to have something
than nothing and fines that would break us!

II

Sun up we'll be out scalloping, slices
of salt water shaving our faces erotic
in the sea's slap, what a groin ache! but
the joy of this life is gone.
It used to be wonderful, the nicest part
of our fishing was returning, now
you're not looking forward to seeing
your family but worrying whether
your trip will be seized because
we counted wrong undersized scallops, we
needed a gross count, then, not a meat count.
You can't judge scallop size until
the shell has been pried open which
kills the scallop so you can't throw it back
in the water like you can short lobsters
to sink into their seaweed nests to
grow big enough for us to come get.
The pried open scallop is dead, no
good to anyone. Lobstermen are
computer scooping our seas while
federal agents armed and wearing
bullet proof vests try
to catch us working outside
their 5 a.m. to 5 p.m. "window" time
frame they schedule us within which

we're watched as if we're not finding
our livelihood but are violating
scallop criminals! We open
scallop shells at sea, weigh the meat
in one pound juice cans, put the meat
on ice in cloth bags stored in our holds
 until inspectors meet the boats.
...we're just fisherman fishing, we're
after fish...we go out and we
work hard. From birth we uttered to
adult remarks that made my old daddy
certain I'd be as good as him in the beds
of the fish of the sea, hear me,
veiled childhood recall, torn away
now by Federal analytical memory
has us loading guns to kill our
repressed lust out of our systems.
We fish...take that from us
our cannibal primal blood will bleed
We only stay above water on hard land
or on boats, otherwise we'd sink
back to our piranha form skinning
skeletons. That's what we do, we
catch fish and part them from their
bones, the scallop from its shell
we are the dead after the dead
we feed to feed.

WET FOURTH OF JULY FIRE CRACKER

We didn't go kill and die in slippery
blood of old men and women, their smell
like rusting sweet plums, to
come home and reminisce.
This is a wet Fourth of July fire cracker, man.
Cool ale house music hums in the bandanna
around the insanity in my cloth circled skull
from death in ankle deep water and helicopters
clucking like spent weapon chambers...killing
children because we feared they'd explode in
our embraces. Sun and breezes fanning us
as we slaughter. Blood pours out of rain
washing wounds. We got missed in the
rat tat FFF-boom! and home
sure we had picked all the blood sucking leeches
off us but there is a wet Fourth of July fire cracker
at Gettysburg...
It's even written in the New York Times...
        "After their 'victory' today
Union horsemen paraded a captured Confederate
banner in front of Federal ranks..."
        And I didn't come home for this, man!
        "Confederates breached the Union line
then fell back... as they did Yankees ran after
them trying to snatch a Rebel battle flag"...
        No, not home for this...on my
Fourth of July too, man! Adults caught up in
enduring fascination of imagining
killing and being killed. We cannot stand
peace and life...We are going to die
and hurrying it is relief.
But the youngsters here barely graduated
out of their high schools into a world that
explodes, are disgusted. I can go into

McDonalds in Gettysburg wearing a
Civil War uniform and people will ask me
which side I'm on where Pickett's charge
north that might have won for the South
was stopped at Cemetery Ridge.
The still agitated Southerner comes here to look
at where resentment and fury is deep in us at
loss of our slaves. The Northerner
comes here because John Wayne would. Ike would.
George Patton would.... "th're-ul Amuricans!"
...either oblivious of or blanking out our Wiscasset, Maine
mansions built of wealth earned Sea Captaining slave ships.
No, man, today real Americans are screaming nightmares.
Now the Draft Dodger and free ride Colonel, fat office boys,
teachers, lawyers who weekend in fatigues for the money,
cocky in exhibitionism and out of the side of their mouths commands
never ever intended to really go somewhere like
we did, hoping not to be bamboo impaled, inured to dying...
...Then poor farmers joined up just for the money
lonely, hungry, nearly starved, ate rats...Slaughter, death
Colonel Higgins strangling for the world,
not some game to reenact.
..."Yesterday a first fight broke out on the
battlefield when somebody dressed up in a
Union uniform unhorsed a man dressed like a
Confederate who seized the Stars and Stripes..."

SONG FOR DYLAN THOMAS

Rip the trees from their roots
like clamped down fingers pressed to hold forever,
rip them loose, as earth unfolds furrows
turned sky's eye exposed to dry hard brown.
Let secure birds shaken from their branches
floundering in the middle of a chirp, burst
forth such singing as only the Welshman,
dripping liquor from the corners of his mouth
bellowed from his lungs until stone buildings shook.
Nor will there be a minstrel from now on,
bard reaching into the hip pocket of his guts
who can come out with one such splendid note
as Dylan Thomas uttered in the snoring of his
troubled sleep.
Sleep, Dylan, whole canyons echo your voice
roaring in our heart's ear forever down the ages.

PROVINCETOWN

I

Something, suction, wind
broke the bird's wings or
slamming a building, now huddled
against the back porch of our motel
blending it seemed in our first casual notice

like part of a stark marvelous painting
of raw death or life of sand and wild brutality
almost bleeding in imagination's vision, this
big old sea gull just against our motel
in Provincetown where grass flushes

dark blush of life faded by
salt along sagging wire slat snow fence
not to divide property but
to control drifting sand.
Here sea has ripped the underpinnings

of the whole cape as ocean
coughed Provincetown out of wind and glacier churnup
to form wild just liveable land mass.
Sky and sea change every few seconds,
colors soothe soft, pink hints barely visible

just before wild nature comes devastating.
Eons ago the sea came up out of the pit of itself
to have a look at its roof the sky and
vomited up a little spread of land to come
and lie on its back and look at the ever

changing heavens as we do, but when it tried
to reel this land back under water it held fast to

its earth perch so now at Chatham
the sea has come back with its teeth
scooping our very homes in big bites

to chew and swallow into the lowest most
belly bottom of its stomach. The sea
wants this land back. See the bright sun.
Fog can come like a threatened octopus,
tufts of clouds low hovering just off the ground

completely disorientating you barely
a mile out of downtown Provincetown. You
have to think, to reason which way
to turn, exactly where you are or must be, sand
has wiped you out but if you just think

you are safe only a few feet out of Provincetown,
think, just retrace...the lit streets...it's...fitting
...these houses little so nature can continue to dominate.
The sun falls into the sea in Provincetown like an invisible big
hand dipping, rinsing a plate...up the Moon!

Night's needle suddenly pricks sun's whole yellow ball
across all wide sky so pink ocean is dark
next to it, red sunset caused by
minute particles of dust off some
erupting volcano in Yucatan.

                    II

Thin Commercial street in Provincetown
crowded summers with tourists
come to get away from crowds to crowd
each other is empty now in this place
where success is the cape has held fast

another day against sea trying to
take back this which it created
in a geological yesterday. Provincetown
where the defeated have run come to hide
and the near dead, the exhausted try

to bicycle, walk, get themselves
back to have some say about where
they die in blinding sunset like
life splattered your blood spread across
the sky before you sink forever and are gone.

Evil and murder were here, lights lit to
lure ships...Home now for
old or sick is called Cape End Manor,
you are graveyard surrounded, fields of graves
seen through all the windows as if beckoning you.

III

Death sings to life here where
life style has no code. Provincetown is open, jazz
in restaurants like 1950's Greenwich Village,
always a horn in your ear, so now blowing
through Napi's wakes your memories...

Herring Cove inland looking back the length
of the cape, a wide screen of the world, sky
and ocean are all one now, almost like
a drive-in theater to see sun go down
as if you were parked to watch the end of the world,

rather than walk on beach like sinking on sponges
to see sunset. Suddenly the whole ocean
is wild lifting itself up over highway to

slam your windshield in sea froth and
leave salt sand caking your car windshield, yet

at low tide the water way out, flat beaches
people are walking on and you can hardly believe
the sea climbed so high to hit you...it's
so far back now...how could could it ever...some
sand dunes, scruffy, look like elongated

female lions sitting on their haunches, tips of
others seem brushed Van Dyke brown, for
a moment there is this great feeling that you
want to stroke them but you'd have to be
a giant to touch them, sand flesh flesh sand so

smooth.. you lose your sense of controlling...
...The sea takes care of me here...I'm still
safe insect size on this little tip...Provincetown,
forlorn, not spectacular, exotic like
California, the Costa del Sol...

                    IV

Here it's struggle, trees scrub pine bent,
twisted against sea driven winds, yet they
grow and they hold and this land is holding too.
Solitude, yet all around us nature is terrible
cruel...out into the water of our motel back

window view are the so innocent looking
stick fences of seines to catch
the fish of this place's life...A dolphin
could be strangling in the tuna nets which
you better not bring up to the local fisherman, these

mammals like us. It's all death the fisherman
think. People die if they don't eat. Death is
an attitude here. Once when we arrived a great
huge sea gull hunched close against the back
porch of our motel where we relish sitting

looking at the view to draw our fatigue out,
restore us but the big sea gull's wings were
broken yet Motel Woman who must have known
she risked our not only checking out immediately
but railing against her place to everyone stood

fast in her shrug, so, a big lovely sea gull
can't fly, has caught death, she pushed the horror
of it out of her head, it was, after all, us
who thought this place Provincetown pretty
and serene not violent to survive.

              V

A guest from Florida kept
correcting me, "it's not a sea gull, too big,
perhaps a cormorant" but it was a sea gull
and no one would help. We were told coldly by
Motel Woman we could feed it if we wanted to,

like, pushing it from herself, how could
we sit and breathe in and enjoy with a
creature of God's dying standing almost silent
weak and not vanishing but Motel Woman,
not wishing to lose customers, put it on us

that at least we could feed it until it
finally gasped and rattled and fell over.
Audubon Society members came all the way

from Wellfleet, and, telling the lady from
Florida where they don't have our

big sea gulls that it was a sea gull,
remarked it probably was too late, the
gull has been standing four days stoic and shivering
against the motel we registered into
in which others stayed and left and left it...

...Next to us in this motel a woman pulled her
curtain across the window to shut out death's
sight come near as a bird, but by protecting
herself during the height of the day when the
beauty was there, she shut out the tremendous ocean

and sky she had come for as well...so this gull
probably would die...sorrow is that it takes
a year for those wings to mend so if the sea gull
lives it can become somewhat tame, confused in
the world of the wild sky and this can be death to it too.

Life is harsh here in Provincetown, only
imagination conjures a lovely Provincetown
in which there is special escape. While we
can pack up and drive away within our
furious mental picture harboring Motel Woman as
ruthless and uncaring, she lives with and loves
a husband broken by the death extracted for
the death of fish, scallops, oysters we chomp on
and slide into our stomachs after the
orgasm of taste buds, as a best part of vacations.

VI

...Way out beyond the whales
the sea coughed up his father's leg bone

three years after local fisherman went down
into the deep sea...They were in an
Eastern rig, net over the side instead

of the stern of a trawl'. They come up on a wreck
and when the net caught they didn't
get fast enough to the winch
so rolled over and
stripped of their flesh by fish

the leg bone of Fisher Motel Man's father
come up in a net of fish catch
brought to Provincetown and identified
by X-ray records as Fisher Motel Man's father
...and the horror of holding

your own father's leg bone picked clean
by the fish you hunt, as you pick
a chicken leg, pork chop, barbecue spare ribs clean
but they're supposed to be things to eat, always
human reckoning is ability to fathom fair is fair but

necessity, these people earn the food their children
eat fishing and scream in horror that God might
want dumb fish to have one of us every few ton.
Fisher Motel Man had a funeral mass said and put
the only thing left of his father in a coffin

into the ground here in Provincetown.
Life where land belongs to the ocean must always
stand off disappearing under water...

While I have no urge to drown
the yearning to return to that ocean
makes me willing to go too if the sea wants me.

...be sure to buy a loaf of bread
and tear it up and throw it out to feed the sea gulls
in case I don't get back to Provincetown.

Curbstone Press, Inc.
is a non-profit publishing house dedicated to literature that reflects
a commitment to social change, with an emphasis on contemporary
writing from Latin America and Latino communities in the United
States. Curbstone presents writers who give voice to the unheard in
a language that goes beyond denunciation to celebrate, honor and
teach. Curbstone builds bridges between its writers and the public –
from inner-city to rural areas, colleges to community centers, children
to adults. Curbstone seeks out the highest aesthetic expression of the
dedication to human rights and intercultural understanding: poetry,
testimonials, novels, stories, photography.

This mission requires more than just producing books. It requires
ensuring that as many people as possible know about these books and
read them. To achieve this, a large portion of Curbstone's schedule is
dedicated to arranging tours and programs for its authors, working
with public school and university teachers to enrich curricula,
reaching out to underserved audiences by donating books and
conducting readings and community programs, and promoting
discussion in the media. It is only through these combined efforts that
literature can truly make a difference.

Curbstone Press, like all non-profit presses, depends on the support of
individuals, foundations, and government agencies to bring you, the
reader, works of literary merit and social significance which might not
find a place in profit-driven publishing channels. Our sincere thanks
to the many individuals who support this endeavor and to the
following foundations and government agencies: ADCO Foundation,
J. Walton Bissell Foundation, Inc., Witter Bynner Foundation for
Poetry, Inc., Connecticut Commission on the Arts, Connecticut Arts
Endowment Fund, Lannan Foundation, LEF Foundation, Lila
Wallace-Reader's Digest Fund, The Andrew W. Mellon Foundation,
National Endowment for the Arts-Literature, National Endowment
for the Arts International Projects Initiative and The Plumsock Fund.

Please support Curbstone's efforts to present the diverse voices and
views that make our culture richer. Tax-deductible donations can be
made to Curbstone Press, 321 Jackson Street, Willimantic, CT 06226.